I0003812

Chapter 1: Introduction to Faceless Digital Marketing for Beginners

Understanding Digital Marketing

Digital marketing is a powerful tool for reaching a wide audience and promoting products or services online. In this subchapter, we will delve into the basics of digital marketing and how it can benefit young beginners looking to establish a presence in the online world. Whether you are interested in faceless email marketing, social media marketing, SEO, content marketing, affiliate marketing, influencer marketing, video marketing, paid advertising, analytics, or branding, understanding the fundamentals of digital marketing is essential for success.

Faceless digital marketing for beginners involves utilizing online platforms and strategies to promote products or services without revealing personal information. This can include creating engaging content, running targeted ads, and building a strong online presence while maintaining anonymity. By understanding the core principles of digital marketing, young beginners can effectively reach their target audience and drive traffic to their websites or social media pages.

Content Marketing Exposed: A Faceless Guide for Young Beginners

Email marketing is a crucial aspect of digital marketing that involves sending targeted messages to subscribers to promote products or services. Faceless email marketing for beginners requires creating compelling content, building an email list, and tracking the performance of campaigns to optimize results. By mastering the basics of email marketing, young beginners can effectively engage with their audience and drive conversions.

Social media marketing is another key component of digital marketing that involves using social media platforms to promote products or services. Faceless social media marketing for beginners entails creating engaging content, building a strong online presence, and interacting with followers without revealing personal information. By understanding the ins and outs of social media marketing, young beginners can effectively grow their online presence and connect with their target audience.

Search engine optimization (SEO) is essential for improving the visibility of websites in search engine results. Faceless SEO for beginners involves optimizing website content, building backlinks, and tracking keywords to improve search engine rankings. By mastering the basics of SEO, young beginners can increase organic traffic to their websites and improve their online visibility.

Importance of Faceless Marketing

In today's digital age, faceless marketing has become increasingly important for businesses looking to reach their target audience effectively. Faceless marketing refers to marketing strategies that focus on the content rather than the individual or brand behind it. This approach allows companies to connect with consumers on a more personal level without relying on traditional advertising tactics. In this subchapter, we will explore the importance of faceless marketing and how it can benefit young beginners in various niches of digital marketing.

One of the key advantages of faceless marketing is its ability to build trust and credibility with consumers. By focusing on providing valuable content that addresses their needs and interests, businesses can establish themselves as industry leaders and experts in their field. This can help attract and retain loyal customers who are more likely to engage with their products or services. For young beginners in faceless digital marketing, this can be a powerful tool for building a strong online presence and reputation.

Another benefit of faceless marketing is its cost-effectiveness compared to traditional advertising methods. By creating content that resonates with their target audience, businesses can generate organic traffic and leads without having to spend a fortune on paid advertising. This is especially beneficial for young beginners who may have limited resources but still want to make a meaningful impact in their chosen niche of digital marketing.

Faceless marketing also allows businesses to reach a wider audience and connect with consumers on a global scale. By creating content that is relevant and relatable to people from different backgrounds and cultures, companies can expand their reach and influence beyond their local market. This can be particularly advantageous for young beginners in faceless social media marketing, as they can use platforms like Instagram and TikTok to reach a diverse audience and grow their following organically.

Furthermore, faceless marketing enables businesses to adapt to changing trends and consumer preferences more easily. By staying focused on delivering valuable content that resonates with their target audience, companies can stay ahead of the competition and remain relevant in a constantly evolving digital landscape. For young beginners in faceless SEO and content marketing, this means staying informed about the latest algorithms and best practices to ensure their content ranks high in search engine results and attracts more traffic.

In conclusion, faceless marketing offers a range of benefits for young beginners in various niches of digital marketing. By focusing on providing valuable content that connects with their target audience, businesses can build trust and credibility, reach a wider audience, and adapt to changing trends more effectively. Whether you are just starting out in faceless email marketing or looking to improve your skills in faceless branding, incorporating faceless marketing strategies into your overall marketing efforts can help you achieve your goals and stand out in a competitive digital landscape.

Overview of Different Digital Marketing Channels

In today's digital world, there are numerous channels available for marketers to promote their products and services. Understanding these different digital marketing channels is essential for young beginners looking to establish a successful online presence. In this subchapter, we will provide an overview of some of the most popular digital marketing channels, including email marketing, social media marketing, SEO, content marketing, affiliate marketing, influencer marketing, video marketing, paid advertising, analytics, and branding.

Content Marketing Exposed: A Faceless Guide for Young Beginners

Email marketing is one of the oldest and most effective digital marketing channels. It involves sending promotional messages to a targeted audience via email. With the right strategy, email marketing can help businesses build customer relationships, generate leads, and drive sales. Young beginners can learn how to create engaging email campaigns that resonate with their audience and drive results.

Social media marketing is another powerful digital marketing channel that allows businesses to reach a wide audience through platforms like Facebook, Instagram, Twitter, and LinkedIn. Young beginners can learn how to create compelling social media content, engage with followers, and grow their online presence. By harnessing the power of social media marketing, businesses can increase brand awareness, drive website traffic, and boost sales.

SEO, or search engine optimization, is a critical digital marketing channel that focuses on improving a website's visibility in search engine results. By optimizing their website for relevant keywords and creating high-quality content, young beginners can attract organic traffic and improve their search engine rankings. Understanding the fundamentals of SEO is essential for businesses looking to increase their online visibility and drive organic traffic to their website.

Content marketing is another essential digital marketing channel that focuses on creating valuable and relevant content to attract and engage a target audience. By producing high-quality blog posts, videos, infographics, and other types of content, young beginners can establish themselves as industry experts and build trust with their audience. Content marketing is a cost-effective way for businesses to drive traffic, generate leads, and increase sales.

In conclusion, understanding the different digital marketing channels is crucial for young beginners looking to establish a successful online presence. By mastering email marketing, social media marketing, SEO, content marketing, and other digital marketing channels, young marketers can effectively promote their products and services, attract new customers, and grow their business. By exploring the various digital marketing channels available, young beginners can develop a comprehensive marketing strategy that drives results and helps them achieve their business goals.

Chapter 2: Faceless Email Marketing for Beginners

Building an Email List

Building an email list is a crucial aspect of any successful content marketing strategy. By collecting the email addresses of your audience, you are able to directly communicate with them and nurture a relationship over time. This can lead to increased brand loyalty, higher conversion rates, and ultimately, more sales.

One of the first steps in building an email list is to create valuable and engaging content that will attract your target audience. This could be in the form of blog posts, videos, infographics, or any other type of content that resonates with your audience. By offering something of value in exchange for their email address, such as a free e-book or a discount code, you are more likely to capture their attention and encourage them to sign up.

Once you have created compelling content, it's important to have a clear and prominent call-to-action (CTA) on your website or social media channels. This CTA should prompt visitors to subscribe to your email list in order to receive updates, exclusive offers, or other valuable content. Make sure the CTA stands out visually and is easy to find, so that visitors are more likely to take action.

In addition to creating valuable content and a strong CTA, it's also important to optimize your website for lead generation. This includes using pop-up forms, exit-intent pop-ups, and other tools to capture visitors' email addresses before they leave your site. You can also create landing pages specifically designed to capture email addresses, with a clear value proposition and a simple sign-up form.

Finally, once you have started building your email list, it's important to regularly engage with your subscribers. Send out regular newsletters, updates, and promotions to keep them interested and informed about your brand. By providing value and building a relationship with your audience, you can turn your email list into a powerful tool for driving traffic and sales for your business.

Crafting Compelling Email Content

Crafting compelling email content is essential for any successful digital marketing strategy. Emails are a powerful tool for reaching your audience directly and driving engagement with your brand. In this subchapter, we will explore some key strategies for creating email content that resonates with your audience and drives results.

Content Marketing Exposed: A Faceless Guide for Young Beginners

The first step in crafting compelling email content is to understand your audience. Take the time to research and segment your email list so that you can tailor your content to the specific interests and needs of your subscribers. By understanding what resonates with your audience, you can create emails that are more likely to drive engagement and conversions.

Once you have a clear understanding of your audience, it's important to focus on creating valuable and engaging content. Your emails should provide value to your subscribers, whether that's through informative articles, exclusive offers, or personalized recommendations. By providing content that is relevant and valuable to your audience, you can build trust and loyalty with your subscribers.

In addition to providing valuable content, it's also important to pay attention to the design and formatting of your emails. A well-designed email that is visually appealing and easy to read is more likely to capture the attention of your audience and drive engagement. Use eye-catching images, clear calls to action, and concise copy to make your emails stand out in a crowded inbox.

Finally, don't forget to test and optimize your email content. Use A/B testing to experiment with different subject lines, content formats, and calls to action to see what resonates best with your audience. By continually testing and optimizing your email content, you can improve your results over time and drive even better engagement with your subscribers. Crafting compelling email content is a key component of any successful digital marketing strategy, so take the time to understand your audience, create valuable content, pay attention to design and formatting, and test and optimize your emails for best results.

Analyzing Email Campaign Performance

Analyzing Email Campaign Performance is a crucial aspect of any digital marketing strategy. For young beginners diving into the world of faceless digital marketing, understanding how to measure the effectiveness of your email campaigns is essential for future success. By analyzing key metrics and data, you can gain valuable insights into what is working well and what needs improvement in your email marketing efforts.

One of the first steps in analyzing email campaign performance is to track metrics such as open rates, click-through rates, conversion rates, and unsubscribe rates. Open rates indicate how many recipients actually opened your email, while click-through rates show how many people clicked on links within the email. Conversion rates measure the percentage of recipients who took a desired action, such as making a purchase or signing up for a newsletter. Unsubscribe rates, on the other hand, indicate how many people opted out of receiving future emails from your brand.

Another important aspect of analyzing email campaign performance is A/B testing. This involves creating two versions of an email with slight variations in elements such as subject lines, call-to-action buttons, or images. By testing these variations on a small portion of your email list, you can determine which version performs better and use that information to optimize future campaigns.

In addition to tracking metrics and conducting A/B testing, it is also important to segment your email list based on factors such as demographics, past purchases, or engagement levels. By sending targeted emails to specific segments of your audience, you can deliver more personalized and relevant content, ultimately leading to higher engagement and conversion rates.

Lastly, it is crucial to use email marketing analytics tools to track and analyze your campaign performance over time. These tools can provide valuable insights into trends, patterns, and areas for improvement, allowing you to continuously refine and optimize your email marketing strategy for maximum effectiveness. By consistently monitoring and analyzing your email campaign performance, you can stay ahead of the competition and achieve your marketing goals.

Chapter 3: Faceless Social Media Marketing for Beginners

Choosing the Right Social Media Platforms

When it comes to creating a successful content marketing strategy, choosing the right social media platforms to promote your content is crucial. With so many different platforms available, it can be overwhelming to decide where to focus your efforts. In this subchapter, we will discuss some key factors to consider when selecting the best social media platforms for your content marketing efforts.

The first step in choosing the right social media platforms is to understand your target audience. Different platforms attract different demographics, so it's important to know where your audience spends their time online. For example, if you are targeting a younger audience, platforms like Instagram and TikTok may be more effective than Facebook or LinkedIn. By understanding your audience's preferences and behavior, you can choose the platforms that will allow you to reach them most effectively.

Another factor to consider when choosing social media platforms is the type of content you plan to share. Some platforms are better suited for visual content, such as Instagram and Pinterest, while others are more text-based, like Twitter. If you plan to share a variety of content types, you may need to use multiple platforms to reach your audience effectively. By matching the type of content you create with the features of each platform, you can maximize engagement and reach.

It's also important to consider your resources when choosing social media platforms. Managing multiple platforms can be time-consuming and require a significant investment of resources. If you have limited time and budget, it may be more effective to focus on one or two platforms where you can create high-quality content consistently. By prioritizing your resources and focusing on the platforms that will yield the best results, you can maximize your impact and avoid spreading yourself too thin.

In addition to understanding your target audience, content type, and resources, it's important to stay informed about the latest trends and updates in the social media landscape. Platforms are constantly evolving, and new features are introduced regularly. By staying up-to-date with industry news and trends, you can adapt your strategy and take advantage of new opportunities as they arise. This proactive approach will help you stay ahead of the competition and continue to grow your audience and engagement over time.

In conclusion, choosing the right social media platforms is a key component of a successful content marketing strategy. By understanding your target audience, content type, resources, and staying informed about industry trends, you can select the platforms that will allow you to reach your audience most effectively. By focusing your efforts on the platforms that align with your goals and resources, you can maximize your impact and achieve your content marketing objectives.

Creating Engaging Social Media Content

Content Marketing Exposed: A Faceless Guide for Young Beginners

Creating engaging social media content is essential for building a strong online presence and connecting with your target audience. In today's digital age, social media platforms have become powerful tools for businesses and individuals to reach and engage with their followers. Whether you are promoting a product, service, or personal brand, it is important to create content that resonates with your audience and motivates them to interact with your posts.

One key aspect of creating engaging social media content is to know your audience. Understanding the demographics, interests, and behaviors of your followers will help you tailor your content to meet their needs and preferences. By conducting research and analyzing data, you can gain valuable insights into what type of content will resonate with your audience and drive engagement.

Another important factor to consider when creating social media content is to be authentic and genuine. Audiences today are savvy and can easily detect when content is forced or insincere. By being authentic and sharing your unique voice and perspective, you can build trust with your followers and create a loyal fan base. Authenticity also helps you stand out from the competition and differentiate yourself in a crowded online space.

Visual content is another effective way to create engaging social media content. Studies have shown that posts with images or videos receive higher levels of engagement compared to text-only posts. By incorporating eye-catching visuals, such as photos, infographics, or videos, you can capture the attention of your audience and convey your message in a more compelling and memorable way. Make sure to use high-quality images and videos that are relevant to your brand and message.

Lastly, it is important to experiment and test different types of content to see what resonates with your audience. Social media algorithms are constantly changing, so it is essential to stay flexible and adapt your content strategy accordingly. By analyzing the performance of your posts and monitoring key metrics, such as likes, comments, shares, and click-through rates, you can gain valuable insights into what content is resonating with your audience and adjust your strategy accordingly. By continually refining and optimizing your social media content, you can build a strong online presence and drive engagement with your followers.

Growing Your Social Media Following

Growing your social media following is an essential aspect of any successful digital marketing strategy. In today's online landscape, having a strong social media presence can help you reach a wider audience, build brand awareness, and drive traffic to your website. In this subchapter, we will explore some effective strategies for young beginners looking to grow their social media following.

One of the first steps in growing your social media following is to identify your target audience. Understanding who your audience is will help you create content that resonates with them and encourages them to engage with your brand. By tailoring your content to suit the preferences and interests of your target audience, you can attract more followers who are genuinely interested in what you have to offer.

Consistency is key when it comes to growing your social media following. Posting regularly and consistently will help keep your followers engaged and coming back for more. Create a content calendar to plan out your posts in advance and ensure that you are providing your audience with a steady stream of valuable and engaging content. Consistency will help you build trust with your followers and establish your brand as a reliable source of information.

Engagement is another crucial factor in growing your social media following. Responding to comments, messages, and mentions from your followers shows that you value their input and are actively listening to their feedback. Encourage engagement by asking questions, running polls, and hosting contests to spark conversations and foster a sense of community among your followers.

Collaborating with other influencers and brands in your niche can also help you grow your social media following. By partnering with others who have a similar target audience, you can tap into their existing following and reach new potential followers. Cross-promotion can help you expand your reach and introduce your brand to a wider audience, ultimately driving more followers to your social media accounts.

In conclusion, growing your social media following takes time, effort, and dedication. By identifying your target audience, being consistent with your posting schedule, engaging with your followers, and collaborating with others in your niche, you can steadily increase your social media following and build a strong online presence for your brand. Keep these strategies in mind as you work towards growing your social media following and watch as your audience grows and engages with your content.

Chapter 4: Faceless SEO for Beginners

Understanding Search Engine Optimization

Search Engine Optimization, commonly known as SEO, is a crucial aspect of digital marketing that every young beginner should understand. In simple terms, SEO refers to the process of optimizing your website or online content in order to increase its visibility on search engines like Google. By utilizing various strategies and techniques, you can improve your website's ranking in search engine results pages (SERPs) and attract more organic traffic to your site.

One of the key components of SEO is keyword research. Keywords are the terms or phrases that people type into search engines when looking for information online. By identifying relevant keywords that are commonly searched for in your niche, you can optimize your content to include these keywords and improve your chances of ranking higher in search results. It's important to choose keywords that are not only relevant to your content but also have a high search volume and low competition.

Another important aspect of SEO is on-page optimization. This involves optimizing the content and structure of your website to make it more search engine-friendly. This includes creating high-quality, relevant content that is optimized for your chosen keywords, as well as optimizing meta tags, headers, and URLs. By ensuring that your website is well-organized and easy to navigate, you can improve your chances of ranking higher in search results.

Off-page optimization is another crucial element of SEO. This involves building backlinks from other reputable websites to your own site. Backlinks are essentially like upvotes for your website in the eyes of search engines, and they can help improve your site's authority and credibility. By building a strong backlink profile, you can improve your website's visibility and attract more organic traffic.

In conclusion, understanding the basics of SEO is essential for anyone looking to succeed in the world of digital marketing. By implementing effective SEO strategies, you can improve your website's visibility, attract more organic traffic, and ultimately achieve your marketing goals. Whether you're a beginner or an experienced marketer, mastering the art of SEO is key to driving success in the digital landscape.

Optimizing Your Website for SEO

Optimizing Your Website for SEO is crucial for any online business or brand looking to increase visibility and drive organic traffic to their site. Search Engine Optimization (SEO) involves optimizing your website in order to rank higher on search engine results pages (SERPs) for relevant keywords and phrases. By following these tips, you can improve your website's SEO and attract more visitors.

The first step in optimizing your website for SEO is to conduct keyword research. This involves identifying the keywords and phrases that are most relevant to your business or niche. By using tools like Google Keyword Planner or SEMrush, you can find keywords with high search volume and low competition. Incorporating these keywords into your website's content, meta tags, and URLs can help improve your site's visibility on search engines.

Next, focus on creating high-quality, relevant content for your website. Search engines like Google prioritize websites that provide valuable and informative content to users. By regularly updating your website with fresh, engaging content that incorporates your target keywords, you can improve your site's SEO and attract more visitors. Remember to use headings, subheadings, and bullet points to make your content easy to read and scan.

Content Marketing Exposed: A Faceless Guide for Young Beginners

In addition to creating high-quality content, optimizing your website's technical aspects is also important for SEO. This includes optimizing your website's loading speed, mobile-friendliness, and internal linking structure. Search engines favor websites that provide a smooth user experience, so ensure that your website is easy to navigate and loads quickly on all devices. Additionally, use descriptive anchor text when linking between pages on your site to improve SEO.

Another important aspect of optimizing your website for SEO is building backlinks from reputable websites. Backlinks are links from other websites that point to your site, signaling to search engines that your website is a valuable resource. By reaching out to other websites in your niche and offering to guest post or collaborate on content, you can build a network of backlinks that improve your website's SEO. Remember to focus on quality over quantity when building backlinks.

Finally, regularly monitor and analyze your website's SEO performance using tools like Google Analytics. By tracking key metrics like organic traffic, keyword rankings, and bounce rate, you can identify areas for improvement and adjust your SEO strategy accordingly. By consistently optimizing your website for SEO and staying up to date with the latest trends and best practices, you can improve your website's visibility and attract more visitors over time.

Keyword Research and Analysis

Keyword research and analysis are crucial components of any successful content marketing strategy. In this subchapter, we will delve into the importance of conducting thorough keyword research and how to effectively analyze the data gathered to optimize your content for search engines.

Keyword research involves identifying the specific words and phrases that your target audience is using to search for information online. By understanding the keywords that are relevant to your niche, you can create content that is more likely to be found by potential customers. This process not only helps improve your search engine rankings but also ensures that your content resonates with your target audience.

When conducting keyword research, it is important to consider factors such as search volume, competition, and relevance. Search volume indicates how many people are searching for a particular keyword, while competition refers to how difficult it is to rank for that keyword. Relevance, on the other hand, ensures that your content aligns with the intent of the user's search query.

Once you have identified a list of relevant keywords, the next step is to analyze the data to determine which keywords are worth targeting. This involves assessing the search volume and competition for each keyword, as well as considering other factors such as user intent and the overall goals of your content marketing strategy. By prioritizing keywords that have high search volume and low competition, you can optimize your content for maximum visibility.

In addition to optimizing your content for search engines, keyword research and analysis can also help you understand the needs and preferences of your target audience. By identifying the keywords that resonate with your audience, you can tailor your content to better meet their needs and provide valuable information that addresses their pain points. This not only improves your search engine rankings but also enhances the overall user experience, leading to increased engagement and conversions.

In conclusion, keyword research and analysis are essential components of a successful content marketing strategy. By conducting thorough research and analyzing the data gathered, you can optimize your content for search engines, improve your visibility online, and better understand the needs of your target audience. By incorporating keyword research into your content marketing efforts, you can create more effective and engaging content that drives results for your business.

Chapter 5: Faceless Content Marketing for Beginners

Creating Quality Content

Content Marketing Exposed: A Faceless Guide for Young Beginners

Creating quality content is the cornerstone of any successful digital marketing strategy. In order to effectively reach your target audience and drive engagement, it is essential to produce content that is not only relevant and valuable but also of high quality. Whether you are a beginner in the world of digital marketing or looking to improve your content creation skills, there are several key principles to keep in mind.

First and foremost, it is important to understand your target audience and tailor your content to meet their needs and interests. By conducting thorough research and gathering data on your audience demographics, preferences, and behavior, you can create content that resonates with them and drives engagement. This will help you establish a strong connection with your audience and build brand loyalty over time.

Secondly, quality content is not just about the words on the page – it also encompasses visual elements such as images, videos, and infographics. Visual content is highly engaging and can help convey your message more effectively than text alone. By incorporating visually appealing elements into your content, you can capture the attention of your audience and keep them interested in what you have to say.

In addition to visual elements, it is crucial to pay attention to the quality of your writing. Clear, concise, and engaging writing is key to keeping your audience engaged and conveying your message effectively. Be sure to proofread your content for spelling and grammar errors, and consider using tools such as Grammarly to enhance the quality of your writing.

Furthermore, creating quality content also involves staying up-to-date with the latest trends and best practices in digital marketing. By keeping informed about industry developments and experimenting with new strategies and techniques, you can ensure that your content remains fresh, relevant, and engaging. This will help you stay ahead of the competition and continue to drive results for your brand.

In conclusion, creating quality content is a fundamental aspect of successful digital marketing. By understanding your audience, incorporating visual elements, focusing on writing quality, and staying up-to-date with industry trends, you can create content that resonates with your audience, drives engagement, and ultimately helps you achieve your marketing goals. Remember, quality content is not just about quantity – it's about delivering value and building a strong connection with your audience.

Content Distribution Strategies

Content distribution strategies are crucial for any digital marketing campaign, especially for young beginners in the field. These strategies help ensure that your content reaches the right audience at the right time, maximizing its impact and effectiveness. In this subchapter, we will explore various content distribution strategies that can help you achieve your marketing goals.

One effective content distribution strategy is leveraging social media platforms. With billions of users on platforms like Facebook, Instagram, Twitter, and LinkedIn, social media can be a powerful tool for reaching and engaging with your target audience. By creating compelling content tailored to each platform and utilizing features like hashtags and paid advertising, you can increase the visibility of your content and drive traffic to your website or landing page.

Another important content distribution strategy is email marketing. Building an email list of subscribers who have opted in to receive updates from you can be a valuable asset for distributing your content. By sending out regular newsletters, promotions, and updates, you can keep your audience engaged and informed about your brand, products, and services. Personalizing your emails and segmenting your audience based on their interests and behaviors can help increase open rates and click-through rates.

Search engine optimization (SEO) is also a key content distribution strategy that can help improve the visibility of your content in search engine results. By optimizing your website and content for relevant keywords, building high-quality backlinks, and creating valuable, informative content, you can increase your chances of ranking higher in search engine results pages (SERPs) and attracting organic traffic to your site.

Paid advertising is another effective content distribution strategy for reaching a larger audience and driving targeted traffic to your website or landing page. By running ads on platforms like Google Ads, Facebook Ads, and Instagram Ads, you can reach users based on their demographics, interests, and behaviors, and track the performance of your ads to optimize your campaigns for maximum results.

In conclusion, content distribution strategies are essential for young beginners in digital marketing to effectively reach and engage with their target audience. By leveraging social media, email marketing, SEO, paid advertising, and other distribution channels, you can increase the visibility and impact of your content, drive traffic to your website, and ultimately achieve your marketing goals. Experiment with different strategies, track your results, and continuously refine your approach to find what works best for your brand and audience.

Measuring Content Marketing Success

Measuring the success of your content marketing efforts is crucial in determining the effectiveness of your strategies and identifying areas for improvement. In this subchapter, we will delve into key metrics and tools to help you measure your content marketing success.

One of the most common metrics used to evaluate content marketing success is website traffic. By analyzing the number of visitors to your website and the pages they visit, you can gauge the impact of your content on driving traffic. Tools like Google Analytics can provide valuable insights into your website traffic, including where your visitors are coming from and which pieces of content are generating the most traffic.

Another important metric to consider is engagement, which includes likes, shares, comments, and other interactions with your content. High levels of engagement indicate that your content is resonating with your audience and encouraging them to take action. Monitoring engagement metrics can help you identify popular topics and formats that are driving engagement.

Conversion rate is another key metric that measures the percentage of visitors who take a desired action, such as signing up for a newsletter, making a purchase, or filling out a contact form. By tracking conversion rates, you can determine the effectiveness of your content in driving conversions and generating leads. Tools like Google Analytics and marketing automation platforms can help you track and analyze conversion rates.

In addition to these metrics, it's important to consider the overall return on investment (ROI) of your content marketing efforts. This involves calculating the cost of creating and promoting your content and comparing it to the revenue generated as a result. By analyzing the ROI of your content marketing campaigns, you can determine which strategies are delivering the best results and allocate resources accordingly.

By measuring these key metrics and utilizing tools like Google Analytics and marketing automation platforms, you can gain valuable insights into the success of your content marketing efforts. This data-driven approach will help you make informed decisions, optimize your content strategies, and ultimately drive better results for your business.

Chapter 6: Faceless Affiliate Marketing for Beginners

How Affiliate Marketing Works

Affiliate marketing is a popular and effective way for individuals to make money online by promoting products or services offered by other companies. In this subchapter, we will explore how affiliate marketing works and how you can get started in this lucrative industry.

Content Marketing Exposed: A Faceless Guide for Young Beginners

At its core, affiliate marketing involves a partnership between an affiliate (you) and a company (the merchant). As an affiliate, you promote the merchant's products or services through various online channels, such as your website, blog, or social media accounts. When someone makes a purchase through your unique affiliate link, you earn a commission from the sale.

One of the key benefits of affiliate marketing is that you don't need to create your own products or services. Instead, you can focus on promoting products that are already on the market and have a proven track record of success. This allows you to earn passive income without the hassle of product development or inventory management.

To become a successful affiliate marketer, it is important to choose products or services that align with your interests and target audience. By promoting products that you are passionate about, you will be able to create authentic and engaging content that resonates with your followers. Additionally, it is essential to build trust with your audience by providing valuable and honest recommendations.

In conclusion, affiliate marketing offers a fantastic opportunity for young people to earn money online by promoting products or services that they believe in. By understanding how affiliate marketing works and following best practices, you can build a successful affiliate marketing business and generate passive income for years to come. So, if you are looking to dip your toes into the world of online marketing, affiliate marketing is a great place to start.

Finding Profitable Affiliate Programs

In the world of content marketing, one of the most lucrative ways to monetize your efforts is through affiliate programs. These programs allow you to earn a commission for promoting products or services on your website, blog, or social media channels. However, not all affiliate programs are created equal, and finding the right ones can make all the difference in your profitability.

When searching for profitable affiliate programs, it's essential to consider your target audience and niche. Look for programs that align with the interests and needs of your audience, as this will increase the likelihood of conversions. For example, if you run a fitness blog, you may want to partner with companies that sell workout equipment or supplements.

Another important factor to consider when choosing affiliate programs is the commission structure. Some programs offer a one-time payment for each sale, while others provide recurring commissions for ongoing referrals. Evaluate the potential earnings of each program to determine which ones offer the best return on investment for your time and effort.

It's also crucial to research the reputation of the companies behind the affiliate programs you're considering. Look for companies with a track record of paying their affiliates on time and providing excellent customer service. Avoid partnering with companies that have a history of shady business practices or poor customer reviews, as this could damage your own reputation.

In conclusion, finding profitable affiliate programs requires careful consideration and research. By selecting programs that align with your audience, offer competitive commissions, and are reputable, you can maximize your earning potential in the world of content marketing. Remember to track your results and make adjustments as needed to ensure long-term success in your affiliate marketing endeavors.

Maximizing Affiliate Marketing Earnings

Content Marketing Exposed: A Faceless Guide for Young Beginners

Affiliate marketing is a popular way for young people to earn passive income online. By promoting products or services from other companies, you can earn a commission for every sale or lead generated through your unique affiliate link. However, to truly maximize your earnings in affiliate marketing, there are certain strategies and techniques you can implement.

One key way to maximize your affiliate marketing earnings is to choose the right products or services to promote. It's important to select products that are relevant to your target audience and align with your personal brand. By promoting products that you believe in and that resonate with your audience, you'll be more likely to generate sales and earn commissions.

Another important strategy for maximizing your affiliate marketing earnings is to focus on building trust with your audience. People are more likely to purchase products or services recommended by someone they trust. By providing valuable and honest reviews of the products you promote, you can build credibility with your audience and increase your chances of earning commissions.

In addition, it's important to diversify your affiliate marketing efforts. Instead of relying on just one affiliate program or network, consider joining multiple programs to increase your earning potential. By promoting a variety of products and services across different niches, you can reach a wider audience and increase your chances of earning commissions.

Finally, don't forget to track and analyze your affiliate marketing efforts. By monitoring your performance metrics, such as click-through rates, conversion rates, and earnings per click, you can identify what's working well and what areas need improvement. By continuously optimizing your affiliate marketing strategy based on data and analytics, you can maximize your earnings and achieve long-term success in the world of affiliate marketing.

Chapter 7: Faceless Influencer Marketing for Beginners

Identifying the Right Influencers

Identifying the right influencers is crucial in any marketing strategy, especially in the digital age where social media plays a significant role in reaching a target audience. Young people who are just starting out in the world of content marketing need to understand the importance of working with influencers who can help amplify their message and reach a wider audience. In this subchapter, we will discuss how to identify the right influencers for your brand and how to establish a successful partnership with them.

When it comes to identifying the right influencers, the first step is to define your target audience and understand the demographics and interests of your potential customers. By knowing who your audience is, you can then search for influencers who have a similar audience and can effectively communicate your message to them. Look for influencers who are authentic and have a genuine connection with their followers, as this will help ensure that their endorsement of your brand feels natural and not forced.

Next, research the influencers you are considering working with to ensure that they align with your brand values and messaging. Look at the type of content they typically post, the engagement they receive from their followers, and their overall reputation in the industry. It's important to choose influencers who have a positive image and are respected by their audience, as this will reflect positively on your brand when you collaborate with them.

Once you have identified potential influencers that align with your brand, reach out to them with a personalized message explaining why you think they would be a good fit for your brand and how you envision working together. Be clear about your objectives and what you hope to achieve through the partnership, whether it's increasing brand awareness, driving traffic to your website, or generating sales. It's important to establish open communication and set clear expectations from the beginning to ensure a successful collaboration.

In conclusion, identifying the right influencers for your brand is a crucial step in your content marketing strategy. By understanding your target audience, researching potential influencers, and establishing clear communication and expectations, you can create successful partnerships that help amplify your message and reach a wider audience. Remember to choose influencers who align with your brand values and have a positive reputation in the industry, as this will help ensure a successful and authentic collaboration.

Building Relationships with Influencers

Building relationships with influencers is a crucial aspect of content marketing in today's digital world. Influencers have the power to reach a large audience and can help amplify your message to potential customers. In this subchapter, we will explore how young people can effectively build relationships with influencers to enhance their content marketing efforts.

The first step in building relationships with influencers is to identify the right ones for your niche. Look for influencers who align with your brand values and have a following that matches your target audience. By collaborating with influencers who are authentic and relatable to your target market, you can increase the credibility and effectiveness of your content marketing campaigns.

Once you have identified potential influencers to work with, reach out to them with a personalized message. Let them know why you admire their work and how you believe a collaboration could be mutually beneficial. Building a genuine connection with influencers is key to establishing a long-lasting and fruitful relationship.

When working with influencers, be sure to provide them with creative freedom and trust their expertise. Allow them to showcase your products or services in a way that feels authentic to their audience. By giving influencers the freedom to create content that resonates with their followers, you can maximize the impact of your collaborations.

Finally, don't forget to show appreciation for the influencers you work with. Thank them for their time and effort, and consider offering them incentives or perks for their partnership. By nurturing positive relationships with influencers, you can build a strong network of advocates who will help elevate your brand and reach a wider audience.

Leveraging Influencer Marketing for Your Brand

Content Marketing Exposed: A Faceless Guide for Young Beginners

In today's digital age, leveraging influencer marketing can be a powerful tool for young people looking to promote their brand and reach a wider audience. Influencers have the ability to connect with their followers on a personal level, making their recommendations and endorsements highly valuable. By partnering with the right influencers, young marketers can effectively promote their brand and increase their visibility in the digital space.

When it comes to influencer marketing, it's important to choose influencers who align with your brand values and target audience. This ensures that the partnership will be authentic and resonate with their followers. Young marketers should also consider the size of the influencer's following, as well as their engagement rate, to gauge the potential reach and impact of the collaboration.

One of the key benefits of influencer marketing is the ability to tap into a highly targeted audience. Influencers have built a loyal following of individuals who trust their recommendations, making them an ideal channel for reaching a specific demographic. By partnering with influencers who cater to your target market, young marketers can effectively promote their brand and increase their chances of converting followers into customers.

In addition to promoting brand awareness, influencer marketing can also help young marketers drive traffic to their website or social media channels. By including trackable links or promo codes in the influencer's content, marketers can measure the effectiveness of the collaboration and track the ROI of their influencer marketing efforts. This data-driven approach allows young marketers to refine their influencer marketing strategy and optimize their campaigns for maximum results.

Overall, leveraging influencer marketing can be a valuable strategy for young marketers looking to enhance their brand presence and connect with their target audience. By partnering with the right influencers, young marketers can effectively promote their brand, increase their visibility, and drive traffic to their digital platforms. With careful planning and strategic execution, influencer marketing can be a powerful tool for young marketers looking to establish themselves in the competitive digital landscape.

Chapter 8: Faceless Video Marketing for Beginners

Creating Engaging Video Content

Creating engaging video content is essential in today's digital landscape. With the rise of video marketing, it is important for young people looking to break into the world of content marketing to understand the key elements of creating captivating videos. In this subchapter, we will discuss some tips and tricks for creating engaging video content that will resonate with your target audience.

One of the first steps in creating engaging video content is to know your audience. Understanding who you are creating the video for will help you tailor your content to their interests and preferences. Whether you are targeting young adults interested in fashion or parents looking for parenting tips, knowing your audience will guide your content creation process.

Another important aspect of creating engaging video content is to keep it short and sweet. In today's fast-paced world, attention spans are shorter than ever. Aim to keep your videos concise and to the point, delivering your message in a clear and engaging manner. This will help retain your viewers' interest and keep them engaged throughout the video.

In addition to keeping your videos short, it is also important to make them visually appealing. Use high-quality visuals, graphics, and animations to enhance the overall viewing experience. Incorporating music, sound effects, and voiceovers can also help create a more immersive experience for your viewers.

Lastly, don't forget to include a call to action in your video content. Whether you want viewers to visit your website, subscribe to your channel, or follow you on social media, including a clear call to action at the end of your video will encourage viewers to take the next step. By following these tips and tricks, young people can create engaging video content that will help them stand out in the competitive world of content marketing.

Video Distribution Strategies

Video distribution strategies are essential for any content creator looking to reach a wider audience and maximize the impact of their videos. In this subchapter, we will explore some key strategies that can help young people effectively distribute their video content and grow their online presence.

One of the most important video distribution strategies is leveraging social media platforms. Young people can share their videos on platforms like Instagram, Facebook, Twitter, and TikTok to reach a larger audience and engage with their followers. By using relevant hashtags and engaging with their audience, young content creators can increase the visibility of their videos and attract new viewers.

Another effective video distribution strategy is optimizing videos for search engines. By using relevant keywords in video titles, descriptions, and tags, young people can improve the visibility of their videos in search engine results. This can help them attract organic traffic and grow their audience over time.

Collaborating with other content creators is also a powerful video distribution strategy. By partnering with influencers or other creators in their niche, young people can tap into new audiences and gain exposure to a wider demographic. Collaborations can help young content creators reach new followers and grow their online presence quickly.

Paid advertising is another effective video distribution strategy for young people looking to expand their reach. By investing in targeted advertising on platforms like YouTube, Facebook, and Instagram, young content creators can reach a larger audience and drive traffic to their videos. Paid advertising can help young people attract new followers and grow their online presence rapidly.

In conclusion, video distribution strategies are crucial for young people looking to grow their online presence and reach a wider audience. By leveraging social media, optimizing videos for search engines, collaborating with other creators, and investing in paid advertising, young content creators can effectively distribute their video content and maximize their impact. By implementing these strategies, young people can attract new followers, engage with their audience, and grow their online presence in the competitive world of digital marketing.

Analyzing Video Performance Metrics

Analyzing Video Performance Metrics is an essential aspect of any digital marketing strategy, especially for young beginners looking to make a name for themselves in the online world. By understanding the key metrics that determine the success of a video campaign, you can better tailor your content to reach your target audience and achieve your marketing goals.

One of the most important video performance metrics to track is view count. This metric tells you how many people have watched your video, giving you insight into the overall reach of your content. By analyzing view count, you can determine which videos are resonating with your audience and which may need some tweaking to improve engagement.

Another crucial metric to consider is watch time. This metric measures the amount of time viewers spend watching your video, indicating the level of interest and engagement your content is generating. By analyzing watch time, you can identify patterns in viewer behavior and make adjustments to your videos to keep viewers engaged for longer periods.

Engagement metrics, such as likes, comments, and shares, are also important indicators of video performance. These metrics show how viewers are interacting with your content, providing valuable feedback on what resonates with your audience. By analyzing engagement metrics, you can gain insights into the effectiveness of your video content and make informed decisions on future marketing strategies.

Conversion metrics, such as click-through rates and conversions, are key indicators of how well your video is driving action from viewers. By tracking these metrics, you can measure the impact of your video content on your marketing goals, whether it be driving traffic to your website, increasing sales, or growing your email list. Analyzing conversion metrics can help you optimize your videos for maximum impact and achieve your desired outcomes. In conclusion, analyzing video performance metrics is crucial for young beginners looking to make a mark in the digital marketing world. By understanding key metrics such as view count, watch time, engagement, and conversions, you can better tailor your video content to reach your target audience and achieve your marketing goals. By regularly tracking and analyzing these metrics, you can optimize your video marketing strategy for maximum impact and success.

Chapter 9: Faceless Paid Advertising for Beginners

Understanding Paid Advertising Platforms

Paid advertising platforms are essential tools for digital marketers looking to reach a wider audience and generate more leads. These platforms allow businesses to create targeted ads that are displayed to users based on their interests, demographics, and online behavior. By understanding how paid advertising platforms work, young beginners can effectively use them to promote their products or services and drive traffic to their websites.

One of the most popular paid advertising platforms is Google Ads, which allows businesses to create text, display, and video ads that appear on Google search results and websites within the Google Display Network. With Google Ads, young beginners can set a budget, target specific keywords, and track the performance of their ads through detailed analytics. This platform is ideal for businesses looking to increase their online visibility and attract potential customers who are actively searching for their products or services.

Another popular paid advertising platform is Facebook Ads, which allows businesses to create targeted ads that appear on users' Facebook feeds and Instagram feeds. With Facebook Ads, young beginners can target users based on their location, age, interests, and online behavior, making it easier to reach their desired audience. This platform also offers advanced features such as retargeting, which allows businesses to show ads to users who have previously visited their website but did not make a purchase.

LinkedIn Ads is another paid advertising platform that is ideal for businesses targeting professionals and B2B audiences. With LinkedIn Ads, young beginners can create sponsored content, sponsored InMail messages, and text ads that are displayed to users on the LinkedIn platform. This platform is perfect for businesses looking to connect with decision-makers in specific industries and generate quality leads for their products or services.

In conclusion, paid advertising platforms are powerful tools for young beginners looking to promote their products or services online. By understanding how platforms such as Google Ads, Facebook Ads, and LinkedIn Ads work, young marketers can create targeted ads, reach their desired audience, and track the performance of their campaigns. With the right strategy and budget, paid advertising platforms can help young beginners achieve their marketing goals and grow their online presence.

Setting Up Effective Ad Campaigns

Setting up effective ad campaigns is crucial for any digital marketing strategy. Whether you are promoting a product, service, or brand, creating ads that resonate with your target audience is key to driving successful outcomes. In this subchapter, we will delve into the essential steps and best practices for setting up ad campaigns that yield results.

The first step in setting up an effective ad campaign is defining your goals and objectives. Before you start running ads, it is important to have a clear understanding of what you want to achieve. Whether it's increasing brand awareness, driving website traffic, or generating leads, having well-defined goals will help guide your ad campaign strategy.

Once you have established your goals, the next step is to identify your target audience. Understanding who your ideal customers are will allow you to tailor your ad messaging and creative to resonate with them. Utilize data and analytics to create detailed buyer personas that outline the demographics, interests, and behaviors of your target audience.

After defining your goals and identifying your target audience, it's time to create compelling ad content. Whether you are running text ads, display ads, or video ads, make sure your messaging is clear, concise, and engaging. Use eye-catching visuals and persuasive copy to capture the attention of your audience and entice them to take action.

In addition to creating compelling ad content, it's important to test and optimize your ad campaigns for maximum effectiveness. A/B testing different ad creatives, targeting options, and messaging can help you identify what resonates best with your audience and drive better results. Continuously monitor and analyze the performance of your ad campaigns to make data-driven decisions and optimize for success. By following these steps and best practices, you can set up effective ad campaigns that drive results and help you achieve your marketing objectives.

Optimizing Ad Performance

Optimizing ad performance is crucial for any digital marketing campaign. Whether you are running ads on social media, Google, or other platforms, it is important to constantly monitor and tweak your ads to ensure maximum effectiveness. In this subchapter, we will discuss some key strategies for optimizing ad performance to help you achieve your marketing goals.

One of the first steps in optimizing ad performance is to define your goals. What are you trying to achieve with your ads? Are you looking to drive traffic to your website, generate leads, increase sales, or build brand awareness? By clearly defining your goals, you can tailor your ad campaigns to meet those specific objectives.

Once you have defined your goals, it is important to continuously monitor and analyze the performance of your ads. Look at metrics such as click-through rate, conversion rate, cost per click, and return on investment to determine how well your ads are performing. By tracking these metrics, you can identify areas for improvement and make necessary adjustments to optimize your ad performance.

A/B testing is another valuable strategy for optimizing ad performance. By testing different ad creatives, copy, targeting options, and calls to action, you can determine which elements are most effective at driving engagement and conversions. Use A/B testing to experiment with different variables and identify the best-performing ad variations.

In addition to A/B testing, it is important to regularly update your ad creatives and copy to keep your ads fresh and engaging. Test different messaging, visuals, and offers to see what resonates best with your target audience. By continuously testing and optimizing your ads, you can ensure that your campaigns are always performing at their best.

Overall, optimizing ad performance is an ongoing process that requires constant monitoring, analysis, and experimentation. By defining your goals, tracking key metrics, conducting A/B testing, and updating your ad creatives regularly, you can maximize the effectiveness of your digital marketing campaigns and achieve your desired outcomes.

Chapter 10: Faceless Analytics for Beginners

Importance of Data Analytics

Content Marketing Exposed: A Faceless Guide for Young Beginners

In the world of digital marketing, data analytics plays a crucial role in understanding consumer behavior and optimizing marketing strategies. For young beginners looking to make their mark in the industry, understanding the importance of data analytics is essential. By analyzing data, marketers can gain valuable insights into their target audience, identify trends, and make informed decisions to drive success.

One of the key reasons why data analytics is important in digital marketing is its ability to measure the effectiveness of marketing campaigns. By tracking key metrics such as website traffic, conversion rates, and engagement levels, marketers can determine which strategies are working and which need to be adjusted. This data-driven approach allows for continuous improvement and optimization of marketing efforts, leading to better results and higher ROI.

Data analytics also helps young marketers better understand their target audience. By analyzing demographic information, browsing behavior, and purchasing patterns, marketers can create more personalized and targeted campaigns that resonate with their audience. This not only improves the effectiveness of marketing efforts but also enhances the overall customer experience, leading to increased loyalty and retention.

Furthermore, data analytics allows marketers to stay ahead of the competition by identifying emerging trends and opportunities. By monitoring industry trends, consumer preferences, and competitor strategies, marketers can adapt their own strategies to stay relevant and competitive in the ever-evolving digital landscape. This proactive approach helps young marketers stay one step ahead and capitalize on new opportunities for growth.

Overall, the importance of data analytics in digital marketing cannot be overstated. For young beginners looking to succeed in the field, understanding how to collect, analyze, and leverage data is essential. By harnessing the power of data analytics, marketers can make smarter decisions, drive better results, and ultimately achieve their marketing goals.

Key Metrics to Track

When it comes to content marketing, tracking key metrics is essential to measuring the success of your efforts. As young beginners in the world of digital marketing, understanding which metrics to track can help you make informed decisions and optimize your content strategy for better results.

One key metric to track is website traffic. By monitoring the number of visitors to your website, you can gauge the effectiveness of your content in driving traffic and attracting new audiences. Understanding where your traffic is coming from can also help you identify which channels are most effective in driving traffic to your site.

Another important metric to track is engagement. This includes metrics such as bounce rate, time on page, and social shares. By analyzing these metrics, you can determine how engaging your content is and how well it resonates with your audience. High engagement rates indicate that your content is valuable and relevant to your audience, while low engagement rates may signal the need for adjustments to your content strategy.

Conversion rates are also crucial metrics to track. By monitoring the number of conversions on your website, such as sign-ups, purchases, or downloads, you can measure the effectiveness of your content in driving desired actions from your audience. Understanding which content is driving conversions can help you optimize your strategy to achieve better results.

Lastly, tracking ROI (return on investment) is essential for evaluating the overall success of your content marketing efforts. By analyzing the costs associated with your content creation and distribution against the revenue generated from your content, you can determine the profitability of your content marketing strategy. Tracking ROI can help you make data-driven decisions and allocate resources effectively to maximize your marketing efforts.

In conclusion, tracking key metrics is essential for young beginners in the world of content marketing to measure the success of their efforts and make informed decisions. By monitoring metrics such as website traffic, engagement, conversion rates, and ROI, you can optimize your content strategy for better results and achieve your marketing goals. Remember to regularly analyze and adjust your metrics to stay ahead in the competitive digital marketing landscape.

Using Analytics to Make Informed Decisions

Content Marketing Exposed: A Faceless Guide for Young Beginners

In the world of digital marketing, making informed decisions is crucial for success. One powerful tool that can help young beginners in the field is analytics. By using analytics, you can gather data and insights about your target audience, their behavior, and the performance of your marketing efforts. This information can then be used to make informed decisions that can drive your campaigns to success.

Analytics can help you track the performance of your content marketing efforts. By analyzing metrics such as website traffic, bounce rates, and engagement levels, you can determine what content resonates with your audience and what doesn't. This data can then be used to optimize your content strategy, ensuring that you are creating content that is relevant and valuable to your target audience.

In the realm of social media marketing, analytics can provide valuable insights into the performance of your social media campaigns. By tracking metrics such as likes, shares, comments, and click-through rates, you can determine which social media platforms are most effective for reaching your target audience. This information can then be used to tailor your social media strategy, ensuring that you are engaging with your audience in a meaningful way.

Analytics can also be used to track the performance of your email marketing campaigns. By analyzing metrics such as open rates, click-through rates, and conversion rates, you can determine the effectiveness of your email campaigns. This data can then be used to optimize your email marketing strategy, ensuring that you are sending relevant and engaging content to your subscribers.

In conclusion, analytics is a powerful tool that can help young beginners in the world of digital marketing make informed decisions. By leveraging analytics to track the performance of their marketing efforts, young marketers can gather valuable insights that can drive their campaigns to success. Whether it's content marketing, social media marketing, email marketing, or any other aspect of digital marketing, analytics can provide the data and insights needed to optimize strategies and engage with target audiences effectively.

Chapter 11: Faceless Branding for Beginners

Building a Strong Brand Identity

Building a strong brand identity is crucial for any business looking to make a mark in the digital world. Your brand identity is what sets you apart from your competitors and helps you connect with your target audience on a deeper level. In this subchapter, we will explore the key elements of building a strong brand identity that resonates with young people in the digital marketing landscape.

First and foremost, it is important to define your brand's values and mission. What does your brand stand for? What are the core beliefs that drive your business? Young people today are looking for brands that align with their own values and beliefs, so it is essential to clearly communicate what your brand represents.

Another important aspect of building a strong brand identity is creating a consistent visual identity. This includes your logo, color scheme, typography, and overall aesthetic. Consistency across all your digital marketing channels helps to reinforce your brand's image and makes it easier for young people to recognize and remember your brand.

Furthermore, storytelling plays a crucial role in shaping your brand identity. Young people are drawn to authentic and compelling stories that resonate with them emotionally. Use your content marketing efforts to tell your brand's story in a way that connects with your audience and showcases what makes your brand unique.

In addition to storytelling, engaging with your audience on social media is key to building a strong brand identity. Young people spend a significant amount of time on social platforms, so it is important to have a presence where they are active. Interact with your followers, share valuable content, and listen to their feedback to strengthen your brand's relationship with them.

Overall, building a strong brand identity requires a combination of defining your values, creating a consistent visual identity, telling compelling stories, and engaging with your audience on social media. By focusing on these key elements, you can create a brand that resonates with young people in the digital marketing landscape and sets you apart from the competition.

Developing Brand Messaging

In the world of digital marketing, developing brand messaging is crucial for creating a strong and cohesive brand identity. Brand messaging is the language and tone used to communicate with your target audience, conveying your brand's values, unique selling points, and overall personality. It is what sets your brand apart from competitors and resonates with customers on a deeper level. In this chapter, we will explore the importance of developing brand messaging and provide tips on how to craft compelling and effective brand messaging for your business.

When developing brand messaging, it is essential to first define your brand's mission, vision, and values. These foundational elements will serve as the guiding principles for your messaging and help you stay true to your brand's identity. By clearly articulating what your brand stands for and what it aims to achieve, you can create messaging that is authentic and resonates with your target audience.

Another important aspect of developing brand messaging is understanding your target audience. By knowing who your audience is, what their needs and pain points are, and how they prefer to communicate, you can tailor your messaging to speak directly to them. This personalized approach will help you connect with your audience on a deeper level and build stronger relationships with them over time.

Consistency is key when it comes to brand messaging. Your messaging should be consistent across all channels and touchpoints, from your website and social media profiles to your email campaigns and advertising materials. Consistent messaging helps reinforce your brand's identity and build brand recognition among your target audience. It also creates a cohesive brand experience that makes it easier for customers to understand and engage with your brand.

In conclusion, developing brand messaging is a critical component of any successful digital marketing strategy. By defining your brand's mission, vision, and values, understanding your target audience, and maintaining consistency across all channels, you can create messaging that resonates with customers and strengthens your brand identity. Remember to continuously monitor and evaluate your brand messaging to ensure it remains relevant and effective in reaching your marketing goals.

Maintaining Brand Consistency

Maintaining brand consistency is crucial for any successful marketing strategy. In the fast-paced world of digital marketing, it can be easy to lose sight of your brand's identity and message. However, by staying consistent across all of your marketing channels, you can build a strong and recognizable brand that resonates with your target audience.

One of the key ways to maintain brand consistency is through creating a style guide. This document outlines the specific fonts, colors, logos, and messaging that should be used across all of your marketing materials. By adhering to this guide, you ensure that your brand has a cohesive look and feel no matter where it appears.

Another important aspect of maintaining brand consistency is through your content. Whether you are creating blog posts, social media updates, or email campaigns, it's essential to ensure that your messaging aligns with your brand's values and tone. By keeping your content consistent, you reinforce your brand's identity and build trust with your audience.

Consistency is also important when it comes to your visual elements. From your website design to your social media graphics, it's crucial to use the same colors, fonts, and imagery to create a cohesive brand experience. This not only makes your brand more memorable but also helps to establish trust and credibility with your audience.

Overall, maintaining brand consistency is essential for building a strong and recognizable brand in the digital marketing world. By creating a style guide, staying consistent with your messaging, and aligning your visual elements, you can create a brand that stands out and resonates with your target audience. Stay true to your brand's identity, and you'll see success in your marketing efforts.

Conclusion: Taking Your Faceless Marketing Skills to the Next Level

In conclusion, as young beginners in the world of faceless marketing, it is important to take your skills to the next level in order to stand out in the digital landscape. By mastering the basics of faceless digital marketing, email marketing, social media marketing, SEO, content marketing, affiliate marketing, influencer marketing, video marketing, paid advertising, analytics, and branding, you can create a strong foundation for success.

One key takeaway from this guide is the importance of understanding your target audience and creating content that resonates with them. By utilizing faceless marketing techniques, you can appeal to a wider audience without relying on traditional methods of personal branding. This allows you to focus on the message and value you provide, rather than on your own personal image.

Another important aspect of taking your faceless marketing skills to the next level is staying updated on the latest trends and technologies in the industry. By continuously learning and adapting to changes in the digital marketing landscape, you can stay ahead of the competition and position yourself as a leader in your niche.

Furthermore, networking with other professionals in the field can provide valuable insights and opportunities for growth. By collaborating with others and sharing knowledge and resources, you can expand your reach and build a strong network of support within the industry.

In conclusion, by applying the principles outlined in this guide and taking your faceless marketing skills to the next level, you can achieve success in the competitive world of digital marketing. Remember to stay focused on providing value to your audience, staying updated on industry trends, and networking with other professionals to continue growing and evolving in your career.

About me.

Meet Stephanie, an incredible individual who has dealt with generalized epilepsy since birth. She is happily married to her best friend of over 20 years and is a devoted parent to three exceptional children, two of whom have special needs. With more than 15 years of experience working for a church, she has served as a youth pastor and worked with young adults. Stephanie firmly believes in the power of love and hard work in relationships. Reflecting on her journey, she wishes there had been a helpful book like this when she needed guidance for moms who wanted to make money without falling for scams. She is confident that this book will empower you to be brave and venture into new opportunities.

www.ingramcontent.com/pod-product-compliance
Lightning Source LLC
LaVergne TN
LVHW081532050326
832903LV00025B/1748